HUSBAND IS NOT GUILTY

(A Research from cases when Husbands were held NOT GUILTY for the offense of cruelty with wife)

ANUJ CHAUHAN

ISBN
Paperback 979-8-89744-625-4
Hardcase 979-8-89777-956-7

CONTENTS

Chapter 3 When Husband is not Guilty — **45**

TABLE OF CASES

(M)

(P)

(R)

(U)

(V)

PREFACE

The legal scenery surrounding matrimonial disputes has experienced significant transformation in recent decades, predominantly with the introduction and application of Section 498A of the Indian Penal Code. Although this provision was enacted with the noble intent of protecting women from cruelty and harassment within marriage, its misuse has emerged as a growing concern. Many husbands and their families have faced prolonged legal battles, social stigma, and financial distress due to false or exaggerated allegations.

This book, Husband is Not Guilty, is an attempt for academic exploration of legal precedents wherein both High Courts and the Supreme Court, have recognized and addressed the misuse of the Section 498-A IPC. Through an analysis of cases where husbands were acquitted/ discharged, or proceedings against them were quashed, this work aims to serve as a crucial legal resource for those unjustly implicated in criminal cases. It provides insights into the judicial reasoning that led to such outcomes and equips readers with potential legal arguments that may be helpful in their defense.

The intent of this book is not to undermine the significance of laws protecting women against genuine instances of cruelty but to highlight instances where legal provisions have been weaponized for personal vendettas. The principles of justice demand that laws operate fairly and equitably, ensuring that no innocent person suffers due to false accusations.

For husbands currently entangled in unwarranted litigations, this book **is an attempt to** offers legal **guidance** that may serve as a foundation for their defense strategy. For legal practitioners, scholars, and policymakers, it provides an academic discussion on the evolution of judicial perspectives on Section 498-A IPC.

I sincerely hope that this book serves as a ideal of knowledge and support for those seeking justice and clarity amidst legal adversity.

Anuj Chauhan

ACKNOWLEDGEMENT

First and foremost, I express my deepest gratitude to Almighty God for His blessings, strength, and guidance throughout this journey.

I dedicate this work to my late father, whose wisdom and principles continue to inspire me, and to my mother, whose unwavering love and support have been my pillar of strength. My heartfelt appreciation also goes to my wife, whose encouragement and understanding have been invaluable, and to my wonderful children, Aishwarya and Arshit, whose presence brings joy and purpose to my life.

I also extend my sincere thanks to Harsh, whose dedication and hard work have been instrumental in the research and compilation of case laws for this book.

I truly appreciate his invaluable support and dedication to this project.

Anuj Chauhan

CHAPTER 1   INTRODUCTION

Section 498A of I.P.C., lays down:—

"498A. Husband or relative of husband of a woman subjecting her to cruelty.— Whoever, being the husband or the relative of the husband of a woman, subjects such woman to cruelty shall be punished with imprisonment for a term which may extend to three years and shall also be liable to fine.

Explanation.—For the purpose of this section, "cruelty" means—

    a. *any wilful conduct which is of such a nature as is likely to drive the woman to commit suicide or to cause grave injury or danger to life, limb or health (whether mental or physical) of the woman; or*

    b. *harassment of the woman where such harassment is with a view to coercing her or any person related to her to meet any unlawful demand for any property or valuable security or is on account of failure by her or any person related to her to meet such demand.*

INGREDIENTS OF OFFENCE.— *The essential ingredients of the offence under Section 498A are as follows:—*

    1. *A woman was married;*

    2. *She was subjected to cruelty;*

    3. *Such cruelty consisted in —*

        i. *Any lawful conduct as was likely to drive such woman to commit suicide or to cause grave injury or danger to her life, limb or health whether mental or physical.*

ii. *Harm to such woman with a view to coercing her to meet unlawful demand for property or valuable security or on account of failure of such woman or any of her relations to meet the lawful demand.*

iii. *The woman was subjected to such cruelty by her husband or any relation of her husband."*

Section 498A of the Indian Penal Code (IPC) introduced in 1983, aimed to address the increasing incidents of cruelty directed at married women by their husbands and their families. The primary goal of this provision was to safeguard women from maltreatment, particularly in circumstances involving dowry demands from their husbands and relatives. It defines cruelty as actions that could potentially drive a woman to suicide, cause serious harm, or constitute harassment aimed at coercing her into fulfilling illegal dowry demands. This legal measure was considered a progressive advancement in the protection of women's rights and the promotion of gender justice.

Nevertheless, Section 498A has faced criticism for potential misuse. Over time, concerns have arisen about its exploitation by some women seeking to resolve personal disputes or apply undue pressure on their spouses and in-laws. Although such misuse does not represent the majority of cases, it has generated significant backlash, often casting a negative shadow over the entire law.

One of the chief criticisms is that "Section 498A" constitutes a non-compoundable, non-bailable, and cognizable offense**. While these provisions were intended to provide swift protection for victims, they have often been manipulated. In certain cases, women have weaponized this law to harass their husbands and in-laws, filing false accusations out of spite or to secure financial benefits. Such abuses can lead to severe repercussions, including damage to reputations, emotional distress, and financial burdens for the accused and their families. In extreme situations, these pressures have even driven some accused individuals to suicide due to societal stigma.

The judiciary has acknowledged the misuse of Section 498A and has implemented measures to mitigate its abuse. In the case of, Arnesh Kumar v. State of Bihar (2014), the Supreme Court established guidelines aimed at curbing arbitrary arrests under this section, emphasizing the necessity for preliminary investigations prior to detaining the accused. The court underscored that the law should not be used as a means for blackmail or revenge.

In a similar vein, the Rajesh Sharma v. State of Uttar Pradesh (2017) ruling directed the creation of family welfare committees to review complaints made under Section 498A before any arrests take place. However, this decision was later revisited in Social Action Forum for Manav Adhikar v. Union of India (2018), where the court acknowledged the importance of balancing the protection of women with preventing the law's misuse.

While recognizing instances of misuse, it is crucial to uphold the importance of Section 498A in delivering justice to legitimate victims. Easing the restrictions of the law might discourage women from voicing genuine complaints. The focus should instead be on ensuring judicious implementation of the law.

Introducing strict guidelines for police investigations, imposing penalties for submitting frivolous claims, and raising awareness about the implications of misuse can help find a middle ground. Furthermore, promoting gender-neutral laws in cases of domestic cruelty could enhance fairness.

In summary, Section 498A IPC remains a crucial statute for protecting women from abuse and harassment. Although the law's misuse by a minority underscores the need for reform, it should not overshadow its primary mission—to protect and empower women in precarious circumstances. A balanced approach that safeguards the rights of both victims and those wrongly accused is essential for achieving true justice.

Section 498A of the Indian Penal Code (IPC), intended to shield women from marital cruelty, has turned into a contentious issue. While its purpose is to defend women against harassment, it has also, in numerous instances, been misused, resulting in men and their families becoming victims of false accusations. What was originally designed to be a protective measure is increasingly viewed as a tool for harassment when exploited maliciously.

Men falsely accused under Section 498A endure severe consequences, including damage to their reputation, financial hardship, emotional distress, and even imprisonment. The social stigma associated with criminal allegations can cause irreversible damage to their personal and professional lives. Innocent family members, such as elderly parents and young siblings, are often dragged into these cases, exacerbating their suffering.

Statistics and judicial comments have brought attention to the misuse of Section 498A. In various instances, courts have observed that the law has been used as a means of extortion or retaliation. The National Crime Records Bureau

(NCRB) has reported a high acquittal rate in cases filed under this section, suggesting that many allegations lack credible evidence.

Men falsely accused under Section 498A experience significant emotional and psychological turmoil. The very accusations can lead to public shaming, social isolation, and strained personal relationships. Many have lost their jobs or businesses due to the stigma attached to such allegations.

Family members of the accused are also affected. Elderly parents, siblings, and even distant relatives are frequently implicated in false claims. The arrest and harassment of innocent family members, particularly women and children, underscore the collateral damage resulting from such misuse.

The prevailing societal narrative, which often assumes men as perpetrators and women as victims, intensifies the challenges faced by men. This gender bias undermines the principle of equality under the law and denies men the opportunity for a fair defense.

To tackle the issue of men victimized by false allegations under Section 498A, reforms are necessary. Firstly, there should be stringent penalties for filing false complaints, including fines and criminal charges for perjury. Secondly, it is essential to mandate thorough investigations prior to making arrests to prevent the undue harassment of innocent individuals.

Additionally, there is an increasing call for gender-neutral laws concerning domestic violence and cruelty. Acknowledging that men can also be victims of harassment within marriage would promote fairness and uphold justice.

While Section 498A plays a vital role in protecting women, its misuse has highlighted an urgent need for reform to safeguard innocent men and their families.

The emphasis should be on ensuring that justice is not only swift but also equitable. Achieving a balance between protecting genuine victims and preventing the harassment of the falsely accused is crucial to maintaining the integrity of the legal system. Laws should safeguard the vulnerable, regardless of their gender, and uphold the principle of equality for all citizens.

1.1. REPEAL OF 498-A IPC AND ENACTMENT OF Section 85 and Section 86 BNS

The Indian Penal Code (IPC), a colonial legislative framework that governed criminal law in India for over 160 years, has been abolished and supplanted by the Bhartiya Nyaya Sanhita (BNS), which became effective in 2024. Among the numerous provisions that have been amended, the repeal of Section 498A IPC and its reclassification under Sections 85 and 86 of the BNS stands out as a pivotal change. This alteration has incited discussions regarding its effects on legal safeguards against marital cruelty and the potential misuse of such laws.

Section 498A was enacted in 1983 to tackle the rising cases of cruelty towards married women, especially concerning dowry demands. This provision stipulated that a husband or his relatives who inflicted cruelty on a woman could face imprisonment for up to three years and a fine. The term "cruelty" was defined as:

1. Conduct likely to drive a woman to suicide or to inflict serious physical or mental harm.

2. Harassment aimed at compelling her or her family to comply with unlawful dowry demands.

Although Section 498A was a significant development for the protection of women, concerns about its misuse emerged over time. Instances of false cases being filed led to the harassment of innocent men and their families. The Supreme Court, in cases such as Arnesh Kumar v. State of Bihar (2014), established guidelines to prevent arbitrary arrests and mandated thorough investigations prior to any coercive actions.

Enactment of Sections 85 and 86 under BNS

Following the repeal of the IPC, Section 498A has been restructured into Sections 85 and 86 of the BNS. The fundamental principles of the law remain unchanged, though some procedural adjustments have been introduced.

Section 85 of BNS: Husband or Relative of Husband Subjecting a Woman to Cruelty

Section 85 preserves the essential elements of the former Section 498A IPC. It stipulates that:

Whoever, being the husband or the relative of the husband of a woman, subjects such woman to cruelty shall be punished with imprisonment for a term which may extend to three years and shall also be liable to fine.

The offense remains non-bailable and cognizable if the complaint is lodged by the victim, a blood relative, a relative by marriage or adoption, or a designated public servant.

The offense is triable by a first-class Magistrate.

Section 86 of BNS: Definition of Cruelty

Section 86 defines cruelty as:

1. Any deliberate conduct that may drive a woman to suicide or cause serious harm or danger to her life, limb, or mental or physical health.

2. 2. Harassment aimed at coercing the woman or her relatives to satisfy an unlawful demand for property or valuable security.

The repeal of Section 498A IPC and the implementation of Sections 85 and 86 under the Bharatiya Nyaya Sanhita signify a notable shift in India's criminal law. While the essential protective intent remains, procedural enhancements aim to strike a balance between safeguarding rights and preventing misuse.

1.2. WHAT IS CRUELTY UNDER SECTION 498-A IPC NOW SECTION 86 BNS

Cruelty defined under Section 498-A of the I.P.C (as it then existed), now section 86 Bhartiya Nyay Sanhita, means any wilful conduct which is of such a nature as is likely to drive the woman to commit suicide or to cause grave injury or danger to life, limb or health whether harassment is with a view to coerce her or any person related to her to meet any unlawful demand for any property or valuable security or is on account of failure by her or any person related to her to meet such demand. The expression 'cruelty' takes within its sweep both mental and physical agony and torture. It is undisputed that the concept of 'cruelty' varies from place to place and individual to individual and according to the social and economic status of the person involved. Whether the act complained of was an act of cruelty, has to be determined from the whole fact and relationship between the parties. The cultural and temperamental state of the life among them are factors from where the cruelty has to be inferred and will depend on the facts of each case. Therefore, to decide the question of 'cruelty' the relevant facts are the matrimonial relationship between the husband and wife, their cultural and temperamental status in life, state of health, their interaction in their daily life which dominate the aspect of cruelty.[1] Views of this nature are found in the Judgment of the Bombay High Court in *Sarojakshan Shankaran Nayar* v. *State of Maharashtra* [(1995) 2 CR 47 (Bom)].

Therefore, the object of Section 498-A of the I.P.C., is essentially to curb the tendency of the unbridled conduct of the husband towards his wife. The provisions are introduced to give protection to the married woman. It is true that a married woman can be harassed, ill-treated by the husband or his relatives in any manner. Some times this harassment drives her to commit suicide, in which case the act amounts to an offence punishable under Section 306 of the I.P.C. But, there are many number of matrimonial disputes which come up before the Courts of law for settlement where the Court finds innumerable difficulties between the husband and wife but where allegation of extreme cruelty is made, it is always the duty of the Court to find from evidence whether allegations of cruelty are true, if so, whether those allegations amount to cruelty as defined under Section 498-A of the I.P.C. There may be instances and instances where the emotional lady may commit suicide the moment a word is uttered in anger or in haste. Therefore, cruelty contemplates the conduct of the husband who intentionally causes harassment to drive his wife to commit suicide or to cause injury to her life, limb, etc. In the absence of any such circumstances, it is difficult

---

1. *Sumangala v. Laxminarayan Anant Hegde*, 2003 SCC OnLine Kar 41: ILR 2003 Kar 1044: (2003) 2 Kant LJ 212: 2003 AIR Kant R 638: 2003 Cri LJ 1418: (2003) 2 CCR 197: (2003) 1 DMC 521: (2003) 4 KCCR (SN 259) 261

to comprehend that such conduct of the husband amounts to cruelty as defined under Section 498-A of the I.P.C.[2]

The husband or relative of husband becomes liable for punishment under Section 498-A of I.P. C., if they subject the woman to cruelty. The offence punishable under Section 498-A has two salient features. Firstly, the cruelty is explained to mean physical or mental cruelty, which has the effect of driving woman to commit suicide or to cause grave injury or danger to life, limb or health of the woman. Secondly, any harassment meted out the woman with view to coerce her or any person related to her to meet any unlawful demand for any property or valuable security or is on account of failure by her or any person related to her to meet such demand is also defined as cruelty.[3]

It is not the intendment of law under Section 498-A of I.P.C. to favour or pamper woman to be dominating and abdurate in the family sans the social and family responsibilities and accountability.[4]

It will be clear from the language of Section 498-A IPC, that if a husband subjects his wife to cruelty, he shall be punished with imprisonment for a term which may extend to three years and shall also be liable to fine. The Explanation under Section 498-A defines "cruelty" for the purpose of Section 498-A to mean any of the acts mentioned in clause (*a*) or clause (*b*).[5]

2. *Sumangala v. Laxminarayan Anant Hegde,* 2003 SCC OnLine Kar 41: ILR 2003 Kar 1044: (2003) 2 Kant LJ 212: 2003 AIR Kant R 638: 2003 Cri LJ 1418: (2003) 2 CCR 197: (2003) 1 DMC 521: (2003) 4 KCCR (SN 259) 261

3. U. Subba Rao v. State of Karnataka, 2002 SCC OnLine Kar 785

4. U. Subba Rao v. State of Karnataka, 2002 SCC OnLine Kar 785

5. *Kantilal Martaji Pandor v. State of Gujarat,* (2013) 8 SCC 781: (2013) 4 SCC (Cri) 448: 2013 SCC OnLine SC 667

1.3. MISUSE

Before we delve into greater detail on the nature and content of allegations made, it becomes pertinent to mention that incorporation of section 498A of IPC was aimed at preventing cruelty committed upon a woman by her husband and her in-laws, by facilitating rapid state intervention. However, it is equally true, that in recent times, matrimonial litigation in the country has also increased significantly and there is a greater disaffection and friction surrounding the institution of marriage, now, more than ever. This has resulted in an increased tendency to employ provisions such as 498A IPC as instruments to settle personal scores against the husband and his relatives.[6]

Instances of a husband's family members filing a petition to quash criminal proceedings launched against them by his wife in the midst of matrimonial disputes are neither a rarity nor of recent origin. Precedents aplenty abound on this score. We may now take note of some decisions of particular relevance. Recently, in a case [7]Supreme Court had occasion to deal with a similar situation where the High Court had refused to quash a FIR registered for various offences, including Section 498A IPC.

Noting that the foremost issue that required determination was whether allegations made against the in-laws were general omnibus allegations which would be liable to be quashed, Court referred to earlier decisions wherein concern was expressed over the misuse of Section 498A IPC and the

---

6. *Kahkashan Kausar @ Sonam* v. *The State of Bihar*, 2022 LiveLaw (SC) 141 as cited in Sikha Ghosh v. State of W.B., 2024 SCC OnLine Cal 1544

7. *Kahkashan Kausar alias Sonam v. State of Bihar [(2022) 6 SCC 599],*

increased tendency to implicate relatives of the husband in matrimonial disputes. Court observed that false implications by way of general omnibus allegations made in the course of matrimonial disputes, if left unchecked, would result in misuse of the process of law.[8]

It was found that no specific allegations were made against the in-laws by the wife and it was held that allowing their prosecution in the absence of clear allegations against the in-laws would result in an abuse of the process of law. It was also noted that a criminal trial, leading to an eventual acquittal, would inflict severe scars upon the accused and such an exercise ought to be discouraged.[9]

' It is a matter of common experience that most of these complaints under section 498A IPC are filed in the heat of the moment over trivial issues without proper deliberations. We come across a large number of such complaints which are not even bona fide and are filed with oblique motive. At the same time, rapid increase in the number of genuine cases of dowry harassment are also a matter of serious concern.

The learned members of the Bar have enormous social responsibility and obligation to ensure that the social fiber of family life is not ruined or demolished. They must ensure that exaggerated versions of small incidents should not be reflected in the criminal complaints. Majority of the complaints are filed either on their advice or with their concurrence. The learned members of the Bar who belong to a noble profession must maintain its noble traditions and should treat every complaint under section 498A as a basic human problem and must make serious endeavour to help the parties in arriving at an amicable resolution of that human problem. They must

---

8. *Kahkashan Kausar alias Sonam v. State of Bihar [(2022) 6 SCC 599],*
9. Sikha Ghosh v. State of W.B., 2024 SCC OnLine Cal 1544

discharge their duties to the best of their abilities to ensure that social fiber, peace and tranquility of the society remains intact. The members of the Bar should also ensure that one complaint should not lead to multiple cases.

Unfortunately, at the time of filing of the complaint the implications and consequences are not properly visualized by the complainant that such complaint can lead to insurmountable harassment, agony and pain to the complainant, accused and his close relations.

The ultimate object of justice is to find out the truth and punish the guilty and protect the innocent. To find out the truth is a herculean task in majority of these complaints. The tendency of implicating husband and all his immediate relations is also not uncommon. At times, even after the conclusion of criminal trial, it is difficult to ascertain the real truth. The courts have to be extremely careful and cautious in dealing with these complaints and must take pragmatic realities into consideration while dealing with matrimonial cases. The allegations of harassment of husband's close relations who had been living in different cities and never visited or rarely visited the place where the complainant resided would have an entirely different complexion. The allegations of the complaint are required to be scrutinized with great care and circumspection.

Experience reveals that long and protracted criminal trials lead to rancour, acrimony and bitterness in the relationship amongst the parties. It is also a matter of common knowledge that in cases filed by the complainant if the husband or the husband's relations had to remain in jail even for a few days, it would ruin the chances of amicable settlement altogether. The process of suffering is extremely long and painful.' [10]

____

10. Preeti Gupta *v.* State of Jharkhand *(2010) 7 SCC 667*

The admission by the sister in law of newly wedded wife, that on returning to her maternal home for the first time after wedding, she did not complain of anything, and told that everything was normal completely demolishes the prosecution story of harassment so far demand for dowry soon after her marriage is concerned.[11]

---

11. *Kumari Chandrakar v. State of Chhattisgarh*, 2006 SCC OnLine Chh 129: 2006 Cri LJ 3822: (2007) 1 AIR Jhar R (NOC 256) 95: (2006) 3 CGLJ 380

CHAPTER 2

ARREST AND COMPOUNDABILITY IN MATRIMONIAL OFFENCES

The Supreme Court of India has laid down comprehensive guidelines in various landmark judgments to ensure the protection of fundamental rights under Articles 21 and 22 of the Constitution. These judgments delineate procedural safeguards against arbitrary arrests, guidelines for preliminary inquiries, and frameworks for handling specific cases like matrimonial disputes. Below is a consolidated analysis:

2.1. Joginder Kumar v. State of U.P., (1994) 4 SCC 260

In *Joginder Kumar v. State of U.P.* (1994) 4 SCC 260, the Supreme Court of India emphasized the fundamental rights of arrested individuals, particularly focusing on the protection against arbitrary arrest and ensuring fair treatment during custody. The judgment reinforced the necessity of safeguarding the rights enshrined under Articles 21 (right to life and personal liberty) and 22(1) (protection against arbitrary arrest) of the Indian Constitution.

The Court laid down clear directives to ensure that arrested persons are informed of their rights, particularly the right to have someone informed of their arrest. These safeguards were deemed essential to prevent custodial harassment and to uphold the principles of justice and accountability in law enforcement.

The Court emphasized that the rights of arrested individuals must be scrupulously protected. The directives issued include:

1. **Right to Inform**: An arrested person has the right to have one friend, relative, or other person informed about their arrest and detention.

2. **Police Obligation**: The police officer must inform the arrested person of this right upon arrival at the police station.

3. **Diary Entry**: An entry in the police diary must record the details of who was informed of the arrest.

4. **Constitutional Basis**: These safeguards flow from Articles 21 and 22(1) and must be strictly enforced.

2.2. Lalita Kumari v. State of U.P., (2014) 2 SCC 1

The Supreme Court of India, in *Lalita Kumari v. State of Uttar Pradesh* (2014) 2 SCC 1, provided clarity on the mandatory nature of registering a First Information Report (FIR) under Section 154 of the Criminal Procedure Code (CrPC). The judgment addresses the balance between protecting individual rights and ensuring efficient functioning of the criminal justice system.

The Court emphasized that while the registration of an FIR is obligatory when information reveals a cognizable offense, certain cases warrant a preliminary inquiry to determine if the offense is indeed cognizable. This mechanism aims to prevent frivolous or baseless complaints, especially in sensitive or complex matters.

To streamline the process, the Court identified specific categories where such preliminary inquiries are justified, such as matrimonial disputes, commercial offenses, and medical negligence cases. By doing so, the judgment seeks to prevent misuse of legal provisions while upholding the rule of law and ensuring timely registration of genuine complaints.

The Court addressed the issue of conducting preliminary inquiries before registering an FIR. Key observations include:

1. Preliminary inquiries are to ascertain if the information reveals a cognizable offense.

2. Categories warranting preliminary inquiry:

   - Matrimonial disputes

   - Commercial offenses

   - Medical negligence cases

   - Corruption cases

   - Cases with abnormal delays in initiating prosecution (e.g., over three months without satisfactory explanation).

2.3. D.K. Basu v. State of W.B., (1997) 1 SCC 416

The pivotal ruling in D.K. Basu v. State of West Bengal (1997) 1 SCC 416 represents a significant advancement in the protection of individual rights against custodial violence and the misuse of authority by law enforcement agencies. Acknowledging the increasing cases of human rights abuses in custody, the Supreme Court of India established a detailed framework of procedural protections aimed at ensuring the dignity and safety of individuals who face arrest and detention.

The directives from this case are designed to promote transparency, accountability, and compliance with the rule of law during arrests and custodial procedures. They require the identification of police personnel, documentation of arrests, notification to relatives, regular medical check-ups, and access to legal representation, all intended to avert custodial torture and uphold the fundamental rights outlined in the Constitution of India.

If these protections are effectively enforced, they will act as a safeguard against arbitrary arrests and custodial violence, fostering a culture of accountability and respect for human rights within the criminal justice system. The key directives can be summarized as follows:

Identification of Police Personnel: Officers involved in arrests and interrogations must display clear and visible identification along with name tags that include their ranks. Records of all officers engaged in the interrogation process should be maintained.

Preparation of Memo of Arrest: The officer making the arrest must prepare a memo at the time of the arrest, which should be signed by at least one witness—either a family member of the arrestee or a reputable community member. This memo must be countersigned by the arrestee and include the time and date of the arrest.

Right to Inform a Friend or Relative: An arrested individual has the right to have a friend or relative informed of their arrest and detention location as soon as possible, unless the witness to the arrest memo is already such a friend or relative.

Notification of Arrest Details: The police are required to notify the next friend or relative of the arrestee, particularly if they reside outside the district, about the time, place of the arrest, and place of custody within 8 to 12 hours of the arrest through the Legal Aid Organization and the local police station.

Awareness of Informing Rights: Individuals who are arrested must be informed of their right to have someone notified of their arrest or detention at the moment they are taken into custody.

Diary Entry of Arrest: A detailed diary entry must be made at the detention facility regarding the arrest, including the name of the next friend informed and the details of the police officials responsible for the custody of the arrestee.

Inspection Memo for Physical Examination: Upon request, the arrestee should undergo a physical examination at the time of arrest, documenting any injuries present. An "Inspection Memo" must be signed by both the arrestee and the arresting officer, with a copy provided to the arrestee.

Periodic Medical Examination During Detention: Arrestees should receive medical examinations by a qualified doctor every 48 hours during detention, from a panel of approved doctors designated by the Director of Health Services in the relevant State or Union Territory.

Submission of Documents to Magistrate: Copies of all relevant documents, including the arrest memo, must be forwarded to the Illaqa Magistrate for record-keeping.

Access to Legal Counsel During Interrogation: Arrestees are permitted to consult with their lawyer during interrogation, though this access may not be available throughout the entire interrogation process.

Establishment of Police Control Rooms: Police control rooms should be set up at all district and state headquarters to ensure that information regarding arrests and custody locations is communicated by the arresting officer within 12 hours of the arrest and displayed prominently in the control room.

2.4. *Arnesh Kumar v. State of Bihar* (2014) 8 SCC 273

The Supreme Court of India, in the landmark judgment of **Arnesh Kumar v. State of Bihar (2014) 8 SCC 273**, laid down significant guidelines to curb the misuse of Section 498-A of the Indian Penal Code (IPC) and to ensure the protection of individual rights. Section 498-A, which addresses cruelty by a husband or his relatives, has often been a subject of debate due to allegations of its misuse leading to arbitrary arrests and prolonged detentions.

To address this concern, the Court emphasized the necessity of balancing the rights of the accused with the need to investigate genuine complaints effectively. These guidelines mandate strict compliance with procedural safeguards during arrests and detentions, emphasizing accountability for both police officers and magistrates.

The directives aim to uphold constitutional principles, prevent unnecessary harassment, and ensure that the power to arrest is exercised judiciously, thereby promoting a fair and just legal process. The detailed guidelines are categorized as follows:

A. **Guidelines for Arrest in Section 498-A Cases**

All the State Governments to instruct its police officers not to automatically arrest when a case under Section 498-A of the IPC is registered but to satisfy themselves about the necessity for arrest under the parameters laid down above flowing from Section 41, Cr.PC;

B. Provision of Checklists to Police Officers

All police officers be provided with a check list containing specified sub- clauses under Section 41(1)(b)(ii);

C. Checklist Submission and Justification for Arrest

The police officer shall forward the check list duly filed and furnish the reasons and materials which necessitated the arrest, while forwarding/producing the accused before the Magistrate for further detention;

D. Magistrate's Role in Authorizing Detention

The Magistrate while authorising detention of the accused shall peruse the report furnished by the police officer in terms aforesaid and only after recording its satisfaction, the Magistrate will authorise detention;

E. Forwarding Decision Not to Arrest to Magistrate

The decision not to arrest an accused, be forwarded to the Magistrate within two weeks from the date of the institution of the case with a copy to the Magistrate which may be extended by the Superintendent of police of the district for the reasons to be recorded in writing;

F. Issuance of Notice of Appearance Under Section 41A Cr.PC

Notice of appearance in terms of Section 41A of Cr.PC be served on the accused within two weeks from the date of institution of the case, which may be extended by the Superintendent of Police of the District for the reasons to be recorded in writing;

G. **Consequences for Non-Compliance by Police Officers**

Failure to comply with the directions aforesaid shall apart from rendering the police officers concerned liable for departmental action, they shall also be liable to be punished for contempt of court to be instituted before High Court having territorial jurisdiction.

H. **Accountability of Magistrates in Authorizing Detention**

Authorising detention without recording reasons as aforesaid by the judicial Magistrate concerned shall be liable for departmental action by the appropriate High Court.

2.5. Rajesh Sharma v. State of U.P., (2018) 10 SCC 472 And Social Action Forum for Manav Adhikar v. Union of India, (2018) 10 SCC 443

In *Rajesh Sharma v. State of U.P.* (2018) 10 SCC 472, the Supreme Court issued key directions aimed at regulating the investigation and trial of cases under Section 498-A IPC (cruelty by a husband or his relatives). Recognizing concerns over misuse of this provision, the Court sought to strike a balance between ensuring justice for victims and protecting the rights of the accused. However, these directions faced scrutiny, and certain parts were overruled or clarified by the Supreme Court in *Social Action Forum for Manav Adhikar.*

The directions from *Rajesh Sharma* can be categorized into several important aspects, including the appointment of designated investigating officers, guidelines for bail proceedings, the role of High Courts, and procedural safeguards regarding the personal appearance of family members. These guidelines aim to ensure a fair and balanced approach, emphasizing judicial oversight and caution in dealing with matrimonial disputes under Section 498-A IPC. However, some of these directives were subsequently refined or set aside in *Social Action Forum for Manav Adhikar*.

The key directives from *Rajesh Sharma* and their subsequent clarifications or modifications from *Social Action Forum for Manav Adhikar* are as follows:

i. Complaints under Section 498A and other connected offences may be investigated only by a designated Investigating Officer of the area. Such designations may be made within one month from today. Such designated officer may be required to undergo training for such duration (not less than one week) as may be considered appropriate. The training may be completed within four months from today.[12]

ii. With regard to this dirction Supreme Court subsequently in the case of Social Action Forum for Manav Adhikar (supra) diected that the investigating officers be careful and be guided by the principles stated in Joginder Kumar (supra), D.K. Basu (supra), Lalita Kumari (supra) and Arnesh Kumar (supra). It will also be appropriate to direct the Director General of Police of each State to ensure that investigating officers who are in charge of investigation of cases of

---

12. Rajesh Sharma v. State of U.P., (2018) 10 SCC 472

offences under Section 498-A IPC should be imparted rigorous training with regard to the principles stated by this Court relating to arrest.

iii. if a settlement is arrived at, the parties can approach the High Court under Section 482 (now 528 BNSS) of the Code of Criminal Procedure and the High Court, keeping in view the law laid down in Gian Singh (supra), shall dispose of the same.[13]

iv. If a bail application is filed with at least one clear day's notice to the Public Prosecutor/complainant, the same may be decided as far as possible on the same day. Recovery of disputed dowry items may not by itself be a ground for denial of bail if maintenance or other rights of wife/minor children can otherwise be protected. Needless to say that in dealing with bail matters, individual roles, prima facie truth of the allegations, requirement of further arrest/ custody and interest of justice must be carefully weighed.[14]

v. This direction was also upheld by the Supreme court in the case of Social Action Forum for Manav Adhikar (supra)

vi. In respect of persons ordinarily residing out of India impounding of passports or issuance of Red Corner Notice should not be a routine.[15]

vii. This direction was also upheld by the Supreme court in the case of Social Action Forum for Manav Adhikar (Supra)

---

13. Social Action Forum for Manav Adhikar v. Union of India, (2018) 10 SCC 443

14. Rajesh Sharma v. State of U.P., (2018) 10 SCC 472

15. Rajesh Sharma v. State of U.P., (2018) 10 SCC 472

viii. It will be open to the District Judge or a designated senior judicial officer nominated by the District Judge to club all connected cases between the parties arising out of matrimonial disputes so that a holistic view is taken by the Court to whom all such cases are entrusted.[16]

ix. Personal appearance of all family members and particularly outstation members may not be required and the trial court ought to grant exemption from personal appearance or permit appearance by video conferencing without adversely affecting progress of the trial.[17]

x. So far as last two directions are concerned Supreme Court held in Social Action Forum for Manav Adhikar(supra) that an application has to be filed either under Section 205 CrPC or Section 317 CrPC depending upon the stage at which the exemption is sought.

xi. These directions will not apply to the offences involving tangible physical injuries or death.

2.6. COMPOUNDABILITY OF SECTION 498-A, IPC

Section 498A of the Indian Penal Code (IPC) addresses the issue of cruelty by a husband or his relatives towards a wife. This section was introduced to protect married women from harassment and cruelty, often linked to dowry demands. Initially, offences under Section 498A were non-compoundable, which meant that once a case was

---

16. Rajesh Sharma v. State of U.P., (2018) 10 SCC 472
17. Rajesh Sharma v. State of U.P., (2018) 10 SCC 472

registered, it could not be withdrawn, even if both parties agreed to settle their differences.

The rationale behind this was to prevent coercion of the victim to withdraw the case. However, the rigid non-compoundable nature of the offence led to criticism, particularly in cases where reconciliation was possible, or the allegations were exaggerated.

The power of the High Court in quashing a criminal proceeding or FIR or complaint in exercise of its inherent jurisdiction is distinct and different from the power given to a criminal court for compounding the offences under Section 320 of the Code. Inherent power is of wide plenitude with no statutory limitation but it has to be exercised in accord with the guideline engrafted in such power viz.: (*i*) to secure the ends of justice, or (*ii*) to prevent abuse of the process of any court. In what cases power to quash the criminal proceeding or complaint or FIR may be exercised where the offender and the victim have settled their dispute would depend on the facts and circumstances of each case and no category can be prescribed. However, before exercise of such power, the High Court must have due regard to the nature and gravity of the crime. Heinous and serious offences of mental depravity or offences like murder, rape, dacoity, etc. cannot be fittingly quashed even though the victim or victim's family and the offender have settled the dispute. Such offences are not private in nature and have a serious impact on society. Similarly, any compromise between the victim and the offender in relation to the offences under special statutes like the Prevention of Corruption Act or the offences committed by public servants while working in that capacity, etc.; cannot provide for any basis for quashing criminal proceedings involving such offences. But the criminal cases having overwhelmingly and predominatingly civil flavour stand on a different footing for the purposes of quashing, particularly the offences arising from commercial, financial, mercantile, civil, partnership or such like transactions or the offences arising out of matrimony relating to dowry, etc. or the family disputes where the wrong is basically private or personal in nature and the parties have resolved their entire dispute. In this category of cases, the High Court may quash the criminal proceedings if in its view, because of the compromise between the offender and the victim, the possibility of conviction is remote and bleak and continuation of the criminal case would put the accused to great oppression and prejudice and extreme injustice would be caused to him by not quashing the criminal case despite full and complete settlement and compromise with the victim. In other words, the High Court must consider whether it would be unfair or contrary to the interest of justice to continue with the criminal proceeding or continuation of the criminal proceeding would tantamount to abuse of process of law despite settlement and compromise between the victim and the wrongdoer and whether to secure the ends of justice, it is appropriate that the criminal case is put to an end and if the answer to the above question(s) is in the affirmative, the High Court shall be well within its jurisdiction to quash the criminal proceeding.[18]

The Hon'ble Supreme Court of India, through various judgments, emphasized the need for a more flexible approach. In *Gian Singh v. State of Punjab* (supra) and

---

18. *Gian Singh v. State of Punjab,* (2012) 10 SCC 303: (2012) 4 SCC (Civ) 1188: (2013) 1 SCC (Cri) 160: (2012) 2 SCC (L&S) 988: 2012 SCC OnLine SC 769

other cases, the Court acknowledged that in matrimonial disputes, including those under Section 498A, the parties should have the option to settle amicably if it serves the interests of justice.

Consequently, Section 498A offences can now be settled with the court's permission and criminal proceedings can be quashed by the High Court under section 528 BNSS (previously 482 CrPC), ensuring that genuine reconciliation efforts are not hindered while safeguarding against misuse. This development balances the interests of justice with the need to address familial disputes pragmatically.

CHAPTER 3

WHEN HUSBAND IS NOT GUILTY

3.1 SECOND FIR ON SAME FACTS NOT MAINTAINABLE

In this case[19] the husband moved Hon'ble Supreme Court against the order passed by Rajshthan High Court wherein the High Court rejected the petition for quashing of FIR filed by the husband. That the sole ground on which the quashing was sought was that this was a second FIR on the same set of allegations made by the complainant after two weeks of lodging the first FIR being FIR No. 19 of 2015 under Section 498A read with Section 34 IPC, Police Station, Hisar, Haryana.

On 18.02.2015 engagement took place and thereafter on 21.03.2015, the marriage of the couple was solemnised at Udaipur. On 10.10.2015, the respondent wife filed a complaint at Police Station, Hisar, Haryana under Section 498A IPC etc. The said complaint was registered at Police Station Hisar on 17.10.2015 as FIR No. 19 of 2015 under Section 498A read with Section 34 IPC. In the meantime, the wife submitted another complaint on 15.10.2015 i.e. five days after the first complaint at the Police Station, Udaipur in the State of Rajasthan on the same set of allegations as in the previous complaint. This complaint came to be registered on 01.11.2015 as FIR No. 156 under Section 498A/506 IPC etc. In the first FIR No. 19 of 2015 along with

---

19. Parteek Bansal v. State of Rajasthan, 2024 SCC OnLine SC 564

the appellant other family members were also roped in. However, after further investigation, a Police Report under Section 173(2) Cr. P.C. was submitted in December, 2015 only against the appellant under Section 498A IPC. Based on the said Police Report, the Magistrate took cognizance and the trial proceeded and a case was registered as Crl. Case No. 232-I of 2015, in the Court of Judicial Magistrate, Ist Class, Hisar.

In the meantime, the appellant filed a petition under Section 482 Cr. P.C. before the Rajasthan High Court for quashing of the second FIR No. 156 of 2015 registered at Udaipur. By the impugned order, the High Court has dismissed the said petition on 06.03.2017 primarily on two grounds. Firstly, that the complaint at Udaipur was prior in point of time than the complaint in Hisar. The second ground was that the Rajasthan Police was not aware of the earlier proceedings/complaint before the Hisar Police and as such the Udaipur Police should be at liberty to investigate the said complaint made at Udaipur. Aggrieved by the impugned order, the husband moved the Hon'ble Supreme Court of India. After the impugned order was passed, the trial at Hisar was concluded, and the Trial Court vide judgment dated 02.08.2017 acquitted the appellant.

Supreme court observed that, It is also not in dispute that in the complaint lodged at Udaipur, the allegations were the same as in the complaint at Hisar and additionally it was stated in the complaint at Udaipur that the complainant had earlier lodged a complaint at Hisar. Thus, the investigating agency at Udaipur was well aware of the complaint on similar allegations being lodged at Hisar. The High Court again fell in error in observing that the Rajasthan Police was not aware about the earlier proceedings initiated at Hisar. The High Court and the Rajasthan Police were expected to at least read the complaint carefully. Thus, Supreme Court Observed, on both the counts, High Court fell in error in dismissing the petition of the husband.

In the facts and circumstances as recorded above, supreme court observed that the wife and her father had been misusing their official position by lodging complaints one after the other. Further, their conduct of neither appearing before the Trial Court at Hisar nor withdrawing their complaint at Hisar, would show that their only intention was to harass the appellant by first making him face a trial at Hisar and then again at Udaipur. It would also be relevant to note that the appellant had been arrested and thereafter granted bail. That in the complaint made at Hisar, there are allegations to the effect that when wife visited the appellant at Hisar, he had made a demand of Rs. 50,00,000/- and also an Innova Car. Thus, the argument that no offence was committed in Hisar but only at Udaipur was also not correct. Supreme Court deprecated such practice of state machinery being misused for ulterior motives and for causing harassment to the other side, thus Supreme Court was inclined to impose cost on the wife in order to compensate the husband and further the FIR registered at udaipur was quashed.

3.2. HIGH COURT TO CONSIDER OVERALL CIRCUMSTANCES IN 482 CrPC and ARTICLE 226

The duty of the High Court, when its jurisdiction under Section 482 CrPC or Article 226 of the Constitution is invoked on the ground that the Complaint/FIR is manifestly frivolous, vexatious or instituted with ulterior motive for wreaking vengeance, to examine the allegations with care and caution is highlighted in a recent decision of this Court in *Mohammad Wajid* v. *State of U.P. 2023 SCC OnLine SC 951.*[20]

Whenever an accused comes before the Court invoking either the inherent powers under Section 482 of the Code of Criminal Procedure (CrPC) or extraordinary jurisdiction under Article 226 of the Constitution to get the FIR or the criminal proceedings quashed essentially on the ground that such proceedings are manifestly frivolous or vexatious or instituted with the ulterior motive for wreaking vengeance, then in such circumstances the Court owes a duty to look into the FIR with care and a little more closely. We say so because once the complainant decides to proceed against the accused with an ulterior motive for wreaking personal vengeance, etc., then he would ensure that the FIR/complaint is very well drafted with all the necessary pleadings. The complainant would ensure that the averments made in the FIR/complaint are such that they disclose the necessary ingredients to constitute the alleged offence. Therefore, it will not be just enough for the Court to look into the averments made in the FIR/complaint alone for the purpose of ascertaining whether the necessary ingredients to constitute the alleged offence are disclosed or not. In frivolous or vexatious proceedings, the Court owes a duty to look into many other attending circumstances emerging from the record of the case over and above the averments and, if need be, with due care and circumspection try to read in between the lines. The Court while exercising its jurisdiction under Section 482 of the CrPC or Article 226 of the Constitution need not restrict itself only to the stage of a case but is empowered to take into account the overall circumstances leading to the initiation/registration of the case as well as the materials collected in the course of investigation.

---

20. As cited in Kailashben Mahendrabhai Patel and Others v. State of Maharashtra and Another, 2024 SCC OnLine SC 2621 (India).

Take for instance the case on hand. Multiple FIRs have been registered over a period of time. It is in the background of such circumstances the registration of multiple FIRS assumes importance, thereby attracting the issue of wreaking vengeance out of private or personal grudge as alleged.[21]

3.3. HUSBAND & WIFE BOTH FILED CASES AGAINST PARENTS OF HUSBAND: DISPUTE BETWEEN PARTIES ESSENTIALLY CIVIL: FIR UNDER SECTION 498 A QUASHED.

In this case[22] the husband chose to institute the civil suit on 27.02.2013 against his family, the wife filed the criminal complaint on 01.03.2013, against her inlaws, alleging demand of dowry and threat by appellants that she and her husband will be denied a share in the property. The provocation for the Complaint/FIR is essentially the property dispute between father and son. Further, the rights and claims in the suit were the very basis and provocation for filing the criminal cases. Supreme Court Observed that the dispute essentially has civil flavour and the allegations in the FIR were vague and quashed the FIR.

3.4. VAGUE ALLEGATIONS

The Calcutta High Court in one case[23] observed that the allegations in the written complaint are general in nature and do not make out even a prima facie case against the

---

21. *Mohammad Wajid* v. *State of U.P. 2023 SCC OnLine SC 951*

22. Kailashben Mahendrabhai Patel and Others v. State of Maharashtra and Another, 2024 SCC OnLine SC 2621 (India).

23. Arun Roberts Rajakumar v. State of W.B., 2023 SCC OnLine Cal 3737

petitioner in respect of the offences alleged. It appears that this case has been filed as a retaliation against the suit for divorce filed by the petitioner.

In K. Subba Rao *v.* The State of Telangana, *(2018) 14 SCC 452 it was also observed that:— "6. The Courts should be careful in proceeding against the distant relatives in crimes pertaining to matrimonial disputes and dowry deaths. The relatives of the husband should not be roped in on the basis of omnibus allegations unless specific instances of their involvement in the crime are made out."*

Therefore, upon consideration of the relevant circumstances and in the absence of any specific role attributed to the accused appellants, it would be unjust if the Appellants are forced to go through the tribulations of a trial, i.e., general and omnibus allegations cannot manifest in a situation where the relatives of the complainant's husband are forced to undergo trial. It has been highlighted by this court in varied instances, that a criminal trial leading to an eventual acquittal also inflicts severe scars upon the accused, and such an exercise must therefore be discouraged.[24]

When on perusal of the impugned FIR as well as the documents available on record and in the light of the judgments passed by Hon'ble Apex Court, it appeared that the allegations made against petitioners are general and omnibus, therefore, they could not be prosecuted u/S 498A of IPC. The FIR lodged by complainant was nothing, but only to wreck vengeance so also with a revengeful intent in order to pressurize and harass the petitioners. Futher in absence of specific allegation of

---

24. *Kahkashan Kausar @ Sonam v. The State of Bihar*, 2022 LiveLaw (SC) 141

demand of dowry or harassment, the impugned FIR was quashed.[25]

Wife registered a case against husband under Sections 498A/323 IPC. After husband got acquitted by the Trial Court, the wife moved the High Court in revision. High Court observed that the petition of wife stated that the marriage between the parties was registered on 13.05.1974 and that she was tortured since then. It has been also stated that the husband left her and later came and assaulted her and has allegedly taken away all papers related to their financial matters.From the judgment of the Trial Court it also appeared that the wife deposed that *"At present she is residing in the same flat which was purchased by her husband but since 2004 her husband is not residing there. She has admitted the fact that she has withdrawn Rs. 5 Lakh 20 Thousand from the account of the husband and she has also admitted she had very less contact with her daughter."* The only other witness for the prosecution knew both the parties. But knew nothing about their dispute. High Court held that there is no evidence during trial nor any materials on record to show that the ingredients required to constitute the offences alleged are present against the petitioner. Admittedly the Case has been filed after more than 35 years of marriage. There is also no evidence of cruelty as defined under Section 498A IPC.[26]

In this case the wife made general allegations. According to her, the First demand of dowry was made immediately after her marriage the second demand was after the passage of sometime and the third demand was made about eight months prior to the complaint filed

---

25. Alok Lodhi v. State of M.P., 2022 SCC OnLine MP 750
26. Sikha Ghosh v. State of W.B., 2024 SCC OnLine Cal 1544

by her. She has not given specific dates and the months when the alleged first two demands were made. Even with regard to the alleged third demand, She has only stated that it was about eight months prior to her complaint. Therefore in these circumstances court held that the complaint contains only vague allegations without details, and without specific allegations with reference to dates. So, on this ground the complaint has to fail.[27]

The mere fact that inlaws might have sympathised with husband accused no. 1 for such demand does not satisfy the requirement of harassment on the part of other accuseds and, therefore, they cannot be found guilty for the offence under Section 498-A IPC.[28]

3.5. RELATIVES OF THE HUSBAND SHOULD NOT BE ROPED IN

It would be relevant at this stage to take note of an apt observation of Supreme Court recorded in the matter of G.V. Rao v. L.H.V. Prasad, (2000) 3 SCC 693 wherein also in a matrimonial dispute, Court had held that the High Court should have quashed the complaint arising out of a matrimonial dispute wherein all family members had been roped into the matrimonial litigation which was quashed and set aside. Their Lordships observed therein with which we entirely agree that: 'there has been an outburst of matrimonial dispute in recent times. Marriage is a sacred ceremony, main purpose of which is to enable the young

---

27. Tarsem Singh v. Amrit Kaur, 1995 SCC OnLine P&H 559
28. *Kodam Gangaram v. State of A.P.*, 1998 SCC OnLine AP 690: (1999) 2 ALD 465: 1999 Cri LJ 2181: (1999) 1 ALT (Cri) 497: (1999) 1 ALD (Cri) 561

couple to settle down in life and live peacefully. But little matrimonial skirmishes suddenly erupt which often assume serious proportions resulting in heinous crimes in which elders of the family are also involved with the result that those who could have counselled and brought about rapprochement are rendered helpless on their being arrayed as accused in the criminal case. There are many reasons which need not be mentioned here for not encouraging matrimonial litigation so that the parties may ponder over their defaults and terminate the disputes amicably by mutual agreement instead of fighting it out in a court of law where it takes years and years to conclude and in that process the parties lose their "young" days in chasing their cases in different courts." The view taken by the judges in this matter was that the courts would not encourage such disputes."[29]

The Courts should be careful in proceeding against the distant relatives in crimes pertaining to matrimonial disputes and dowry deaths. The relatives of the husband should not be roped in on the basis of omnibus allegations unless specific instances of their involvement in the crime are made out.[30]

High Court brought it to the notice of learned Addl. SPP that in many of the transactions under Sections 498A, 304B and 306 IPC i.e. the cases where serious matrimonial offences are alleged that the police have been indiscriminately roping-in the whole of the family including the brothers, sisters, in laws. Unless there is specific material against these persons it is downright wrong on the part of the investigating authorities to indiscriminately include the whole of the family as accused persons. There could possibly be strong evidence against the husband or parents

---

29. As cited in *Geeta Mehrotra v. State of UP; (2012) 10 SCC 741*
30. *K. Subba Rao v. The State of Telangana, (2018) 14 SCC 452*

or immediate residents of the house etc., but the police need to discriminate before just adding the whole of the family as accused persons as has happened in this case.[31]

3.6. ORDINARY WEAR AND TEAR IN MATRIMONIAL LIFE DOES NOT AMOUNT TO CRUELTY

There will be ordinary wear and tear in any matrimonial life but that does not amount to cruelty or harassment. It is settled law that every type of harassment or every type of cruelty, would not attract Section 498A or Section 306 of IPC. It must be established that the harassment or cruelty was with a view to force the wife to commit suicide or to fulfill illegal demands of husband or in-laws. The witnesses have given evidence of harassment only on the basis of what the deceased Swati is supposed to have told them. The deceased Swati was married for 8 years but P.W.-2 did not feel it was necessary to report the matter to the police even once. In the present case, the allegations against Accused was not that Swati was subjected to cruelty on account of any illegal demand. Except bare words of the witnesses that Swati used to complain about harassment, there is no other positive evidence on cruelty. When Swati committed suicide, Accused Nos. 2 to 4 were residing at Village Surpur and they came from village Surpur on receiving information about the commission of suicide by Swati. There is no evidence to show that the Accused in any way instigated or aided Swati to commit suicide. Therefore, the Trial Court has rightly concluded that on the face of records, there is no evidence

---

31. State vs Srikanth and ors., 2002 SCC OnLine Kar 351: ILR 2002 Kar 3469: (2002) 5 Kant LJ 191 (DB): 2002 Cri LJ 3605: (2002) 2 HLR 618 (DB): (2003) 1 DMC 268: (2002) 3 KCCR 2095

to conclude that the Accused in any way abetted the commission of suicide.[32]

Cruelty under Section 498A means any willful conduct which is of such nature as is likely to drive the woman to commit suicide. It also means harassment of the woman where such harassment is with a view to coercing her or any person related to her to meet any unlawful demand for any property or valuable security or is on account of failure by her or any person related to her to meet such demand. Therefore, the prosecution has to prove a willful conduct, which is of such nature as is likely to drive the woman to commit suicide. No such willful conduct has been established because none of the witnesses have given evidence to have seen the Accused indulging in such willful conduct that could drive a woman to commit suicide. Moreover, if a woman is harassed, that harassment should be with a view to coercing her or any person related to her to meet any unlawful demand for any property or valuable security, or is on account of failure by her or any person related to her to meet such demand. Therefore, the prosecution has to prove that there was any unlawful demand for any property or valuable security by the Accused. None of the witnesses have stated that there was any such demand by the Accused. Therefore, the charge under Section 498A cannot stick.[33]

Under Section 306, any person who abets the commission of suicide shall be punished with imprisonment and fine, as the court may decide. Abetment involves a

---

32. STATE OF MAHARASHTRA V. ANIL KURKOTTI, 2019 SCC ONLINE BOM 4508

33. STATE OF MAHARASHTRA V. ANIL KURKOTTI, 2019 SCC ONLINE BOM 4508

mental process of instigating a person in doing something. A person abets the doing of a thing when he instigates any person to do that thing or engages one or more persons in any conspiracy for the doing of that thing or he intentionally aids, by acts or illegal omission, the doing of that thing. These are essential to complete the abetment as a crime. The word instigate literally means to provoke, incite, urge on or bring about by persuasion to do anything. Section 113A of the Indian Evidence Act requires that there must be material to show that the victim was subjected to cruelty or harassment and then there can be a presumption of abetment. The prosecution has not proved any where the harassment or any willful conduct that drove the woman to commit suicide.[34]

The taking of drink and coming home late much against the will of the wife may not per se amount to cruelty under sec 498A ipc.[35]

3.7. HAVING DOUBT IN MIND ABOUT CHARACTER OF WIFE NOT SUFFICIENT TO ATTRACT OFFENCE U/S 498-A, 306 IPC

The husband belonged to a scheduled tribe of Adivasi. He was young man of hardly 22 years old and doing the labour work. He got married with one "Manjula", hardly aged 18 years. She committed suicide by hanging herself at her in-laws house on 15-4-1991 at about 11.30 p.m. allegedly because of the mental cruelty meted out to her by her husband. It was the case of the prosecution that her husband was having doubt about her character,

---

34. STATE OF MAHARASHTRA V. ANIL KURKOTTI, 2019 SCC ONLINE BOM 4508

35. Bikshapathi vs state of andra Pradesh 1989 CRLJ 1186 (AP)

therefore, he was talking less with her and because of that she committed suicide. Thus, the husband was accused of having committed an offence u/Section 498-A (Cruelty with wife) and Section 306 (Abetment to suicide) I.P.C.

After careful consideration the Gujrat High Court observed that even assuming for the sake of argument that the appellant-accused was having doubt in his mind about his wife eloped with some one for a particular period that itself would not be sufficient to hold him guilty for the offences, either punishable u/Sections 498-A or 306 I.P.C. In the instant case the allegations against the appellant-accused was that because he was having doubt in his mind, therefore, he was talking rarely with his wife. Such an act of accused cannot be considered to be an abetment.[36]

3.8. USUAL AND COMMON DOMESTIC DISCORD IN ANY MATRIMONIAL HOME CANNOT AMOUNT TO 'CRUELTY'

According to the prosecution, the Appellant (Mother in Law) subjected the deceased (wife) to mental cruelty by making her do all the household work by herself. She was to collect grass for the cow; they also asked her to bring water from the "Oli". She was also made to wash the cloths of her father-in-law, mother-in-law and sister-in-law, who were residing in the house. The appellant used to find fault with the deceased for all works and actions done by her. She was not allowed to have free phone calls to her husband stating

---

36. *Rameshbhai Dalaji Godad v. State of Gujarat,* 2003 SCC OnLine Guj 15: (2003) 2 GLH 657: (2003) 44 (3) GLR 2390: 2003 Cri LJ 2445: (2004) 3 CCR 296: (2003) 2 DMC 746: (2004) 2 DMC 124 at page 658

that phone bill would increase and that if she wanted to talk more, she should bring more money from her house. Thus, according to the prosecution, the mental cruelty meted out to the deceased was intolerable and because of the cruel treatment mentioned above, she committed suicide by hanging.

High Court observed that the usual and common domestic discord in any matrimonial home cannot amount to 'cruelty' within the meaning of Section 498 A of IPC. Such act or wilful conduct must be one which must drive the woman to commit suicide. The standard of tolerance of a woman may vary from person to person. One woman may be so hyper sensitive that even a simple innocuous and harmless statement may be taken by her as a serious one. Similarly, the directions, instructions or comments made by an elder member of the family to do or not to do a particular work or showing or stating about the mistakes may not be taken in the proper or right sense. Therefore, it all depends upon the person to whom it was said.[37]

The Supreme Court has very clearly elucidated the interlinking between these two offences but what we also need to take note of is that the very definition of Section 498-A of the IPC and the case law clearly postulates that the evidence of cruelty is required to be established, cruelty of a grave level which is sufficient to seriously jeopardise the mental or physical well-being of the spouse. The law does not contemplate the usual day-to-day misunderstandings or quarrels or minor matrimonial problems which do not have this kind of after-effects.[38]

---

37. Rosamma Kurian v. State of Kerala, 2014 SCC OnLine Ker 2712
38. *State by C.O.D. Police, Anti Dowry Cell, Bangalore v. K. Sridhar*, 1999 SCC OnLine Kar 353: (2000) 1 Kant LJ 274: 2000 Cri LJ 328: (2000) 1 DMC 320

Even if, it be assumed that a demand of Rs. 15,000/- was made by from father or mother of the deceased wife, such mere demand will not bring the case either within the ambit of Sec. 304-B or Sec. 498-A, Penal Code, 1860, in the absence of evidence that the deceased was being, treated with cruelty on account of such, demand.[39]

3.9. NO CRUELTY MADE ON PETTY QUARELLS AND OMNIBUS ALLEGATIONS

In the evidence of parents of deceased wife it came that deceased informed them about the ill-treatment and the behaviour of the accused. Nothing was spoken as to what was that ill-treatment and the behaviour of the appellant. The allegation made in the complaint was that the appellant evinced interest in political activities and was addicted to alcohol and used to ill-treat the deceased by beating, insulting and demanding her to bring the money. Andhra Pradesh High Court observed that the ill-treatment of the appellant should come within the meaning of cruelty and has to be sound, hence, evincing interest in political activities, and the omnibus allegation such as the appellant was ill-treating the deceased by beating, insulting and demanding her to bring money would not come within the meaning of cruelty as defined under Section 498-A IPC. In any marital life, it cannot be said that there was total harmony and it is not uncommon between the wife and husband to have some petty quarrels, which in my considered view, cannot be termed as 'cruelty' to attract the provisions of Section 498-A IPC.[40]

---

39. *State of Himachal Pradesh v. Yog Raj*, 1996 SCC OnLine HP 60: 1997 Cri LJ 2033: (1997) 2 HLR 39: (1996) 2 Ch LR 378
40. *Vadala Vinay Kumar v. State of A.P.*, 2006 SCC OnLine AP 5: (2006) 1 AP LJ 375: (2006) 4 AIR Bom R (NOC 585) 5: 2006 Cri LJ 1710: (2006) 1 ALT (Cri) 437: (2006) 1 ALD (Cri) 530

One instance unless portentous, in the absence of any material evidence of interference and involvement in the marital life of the complainant, may not be sufficient to implicate the person as having committed cruelty under section 498A of the IPC.[41]

3.10. LONG GAP BETWEEN ALLEGED CRUELTY AND SUICIDE

When there was a gap of three to four years between the alleged incidents of cruelty and the suicide by the wife, the High Court observed the evidence was rather on the weak side but will also not be of much assistance to the prosecution even assuming it is accepted, because the point of time when the incident has taken place in so far remote i.e. there is a gap of 3 to 4 years between these incident and the suicide that has subsequently transpired and consequently, Court was of the view that the nexus or interconnection between the two has not been established.[42]

3.11. NECESSITY OF CRIMINAL INTENT

After going through evidence of complainant, Bombay High Court observed, it does not appear that she has conclusively established that the beating and harassment was with a view to force her to commit suicide or to fulfil the illegal demands of the non-applicants. The trial Court

---

41. MAHALAKSHMI vs. THE STATE OF KARNATAKA., Supree Court of India, Diary No.- 13940 – 2019, 2023 LiveLaw(SC) 1041

42. State vs Srikanth and ors., 2002 SCC OnLine Kar 351: ILR 2002 Kar 3469: (2002) 5 Kant LJ 191 (DB): 2002 Cri LJ 3605: (2002) 2 HLR 618 (DB): (2003) 1 DMC 268: (2002) 3 KCCR 2095

has discussed this aspect at some length and has recorded a finding that offence under Section 498-A, Penal Code, 1860, is not established. Bombay High Court refused to interfere with the order of Trial Court at the instance of the complainant, particularly when the State has not challenged the impugned order.[43]

3.12. NOT CALLING WIFE FROM HER PARENTAL HOME IS NOT HARASSMENT

In this case High Court observed that cruelty must be one which is likely to cause grave injury or danger to life, limb or health (of course, either mental or physical) of the woman. The mere statement that the woman had fallen ill may not constitute cruelty within the meaning of section 498A of the Penal Code, 1860 unless the illness, either mental or physical, is of such nature as to cause grave injury or danger to life, limb or health. Similarly the harassment must also be such as should have been actually meted out by the accused. **Simply because the husband and others did not call the wife to the matrimonial home, it cannot amount to harassment.** Driving her out from the matrimonial home to her perental home will be harassment, but not calling her back to the marital home cannot amount to harassment, although the husband at the worst can be stated to be guilty of desertion if he makes the stay of the wife in the marital home unsafe and, therefore, makes her to leave matrimonial home.[44]

---

43. Sarla Prabhakar Waghmare v. State of Maharashtra and ors., 1989 SCC OnLine Bom 355: 1990 Cri LJ 407: (1990) 1 AP LJ (DNC) 55: (1991) 1 HLR 438: (1991) 1 DMC 310
44. Tarsem Singh v. Amrit Kaur, 1995 SCC OnLine P&H 559

3.13. COMPLAINT LIES IN THE JURISDICTION OF COURT WHERE CRUELTY ACTUALLY TOOK PLACE

Holding that it husband is not guilty of harassment by not calling her to the marital home and thereby clothe the magistrate's court, within whose local jurisdiction the house of her parents is situated, with jurisdiction to entertain a complaint by her under S. 498-A, IPC. In these circumstances, High Court held that no part of the alleged cruelty or harassment arose within the jurisdiction of the Court of Judicial Magistrate at Batala and, therefore, the court at Batala has no jurisdiction to entertain this complaint against the petitioners herein under Section 498-A, Penal Code, 1860. The result is that the complaint, the summoning order and the proceedings emanating therefrom will have to be quashed.[45]

3.14. CRIMINAL INTENT NECESSARY

When wife could not conclusively establish that the beating and harassment was with a view to force her to commit suicide or to fulfil the illegal demands of the non-applicants. The trial court held that offence under 498 A is not attracted and the decision of trial court was upheld by High Court.[46]

It has been held by this Court in *C. Veerudu* v. *State of A.P.*, (1988) 2 Andh LT 171: (1989 Cri LJ NOC 52) that even in respect of the offence under Section 498-A, IPC, the necessary mens rea is required.[47]

---

45. Tarsem Singh v. Amrit Kaur, 1995 SCC OnLine P&H 559

46. *Sarla Prabhakar Waghmare v. State of Maharashtra*, 1989 SCC OnLine Bom 355: 1990 Cri LJ 407: (1990) 1 AP LJ (DNC) 55: (1991) 1 HLR 438: (1991) 1 DMC 310

47. As cited in *Ch. Narender Reddy v. State of A.P.*, 2000 SCC OnLine AP 766: 2000 Cri LJ 4068

3.15 A MERE BEATING ON ONE OCCASION

In this case the allegation against the husband was that he poured kerosene on the person of his wife and killed her by fire. In the evidence recorded it was found that there were no traces of kerosene in the room etc. High Court observed, if really the accused had poured kerosene on the person of the deceased and had set fire, there should be kerosene on the floor of the kitchen room where the deceased was lying after the accident. It is further stated that immediately after the accident the deceased was shifted in an auto to the Hospital. In such a case the body and clothes of the deceased should be smelling kerosene. However, the Doctor opined that there is no smell of kerosene. This indicates that no kerosene is poured on the body of the deceased and no force is used against the deceased at the time of the incident. Therefore, the circumstances in this case are more in favour of the accidental death rather than suicidal or homicidal death. Further the High Court held that a mere beating on one occasion is not sufficient to constitute cruelty under Section 498-A I.P.C.[48]

3.16. HUSBAND TAKING AWAY CHILD FROM CUSTODY OF MOTHER

When wife contended that forcibly taking away the minor child from the custody of the mother amounts to cruelty as defined under Section 498-A of the I.P.C. High Court observed that where differences arose between the husband and wife, specially where the disgruntled

---

48. *Jaya Sankara Rao v. State of A.P.*, 1996 SCC OnLine AP 126: (1996) 1 AP LJ 404: (1996) 2 ALD 263: (1997) 1 HLR 219: (1996) 1 ALT (Cri) 560: (1996) 1 ALD (Cri) 507: (1996) 2 DMC 625

parties have an issue and that minor child is in the custody of father or mother, invariably the other spouse throngs for the custody of the child. It is intense in the case of the mother. Law has provided-sufficient means to secure the custody of the minor child and the Courts have to decide that question on the merits of each case. Therefore, where a father of the minor takes away his child from the custody of the mother even without informing her and who is legally entitled for the custody of the child, that act does not amount to subjecting her to cruelty for the purpose of Section 498-A of the I.P.C.[49]

3.17.　SECTION 498-A of I.P.C. IS NOT TO PAMPER TO BE DOMINATING AND ABDURATE

In this case the allegation against husband and is family was that they told the deceased wife not to visit kitchen in order to prevent wastage. It was therefore pleaded that accused persons have committed offence under section 498 A IPC as this conduct had driven the wife to commit suicide. Considering the facts of the case the High Court observed, It is not the intendment of law under Section 498-A of I.P.C. to favour or pamper woman to be dominating and abdurate in the family sans the social and family responsibilities and accountability. Merely, because her in-laws or husband were to chastise woman for improper or immoral conduct, it does not necessarily amounts to cruelty. It appears that the deceased is hyper-sensitive lady not used to usual wear and tear of social life and

---

49. *Sumangala v. Laxminarayan Anant Hegde*, 2003 SCC OnLine Kar 41: ILR 2003 Kar 1044: (2003) 2 Kant LJ 212: 2003 AIR Kant R 638: 2003 Cri LJ 1418: (2003) 2 CCR 197: (2003) 1 DMC 521: (2003) 4 KCCR (SN 259) 261

does not have flexible temperamental compatibility to the changing circumstances of life. The accused persons appear to be modest and thrifty persons. The deceased perhaps indulging in wastage of material in the kitchen. Therefore, they might have chastised the deceased and told her not to attend the kitchen to prevent the wastage. Such conduct on the part of the appellants cannot be construed as one which is likely to drive the deceased to commit suicide and it is only in the nature of censure or mild reprimand not amounting to cruelty. The appellants-accused were therefore acquitted.[50]

3.18. GROUND RAISED BY HUSBAND IN DIVORCE PETITION CAN NOT BE BASIS OF CRUELTY

In this case High Court observed that the allegations raised by the revision petitioner seeking divorce when ultimately turned to be baseless resulting in dismissal of the divorce petition, ultimately amount to cruelty cannot for a moment be accepted. The main allegation made by the revision petitioner while seeking divorce is that the wife was suffering from virulent disease like Cancer. It is unheard of in legal parlance that such a ground raised by the husband seeking divorce against the wife amounts to legal cruelty. It cannot be said by any stretch of imagination that the ground mentioned in the Divorce petition that the wife was suffering from Cancer, if ultimately considered to be a cruelty for a moment, the necessary mens rea is lacking, which is a necessary ingredient, so as to bring home the offence under S. 498-A, IPC.[51]

---

50. U. Subba Rao v. State of Karnataka, 2002 SCC OnLine Kar 785
51. *Ch. Narender Reddy v. State of A.P.*, 2000 SCC OnLine AP 766: 2000 Cri LJ 4068

3.19. HUSBAND HAVING FRIENDSHIP WITH OTHER GIRL

In this case High Court observed that there is also a charge that the accused was friendly with one M and that this is also one of the aspects of cruelty *vis-a-vis* the wife who had reacted seriously to this. That allegation is only in the form of a suggestion and M, who was even cited as a witness was not examined. More importantly, what we find on a very minute evaluation of the record is that a review of the incident would undoubtedly disclose some level of unhappiness to the deceased, but in order to establish the criminal offence under either or both of the charges the incidence, gravity and the volume of the cruelty would have to be much higher. All that we can hold is that this material comes dangerously close, but that in its totality, it is not good enough to sustain a conviction under either of the two charges.[52]

3.20. HUSBAND NOT PREPARED TO LIVE SEPARATELY WITH WIFE

In this case the deceased wife wrote a dying declaration. The only grievance made in the dying declaration was that she wanted to live separately but her husband was not prepared and on that score, the husband had beaten her in the afternoon on the day prior to the day of incident. It was then stated therein that her grandmother disliked her. High Court held that these statements in the dying declaration, were not sufficient to substantiate the prosecution case

---

52. *State by C.O.D. Police, Anti Dowry Cell, Bangalore v. K. Sridhar*, 1999 SCC OnLine Kar 353: (2000) 1 Kant LJ 274: 2000 Cri LJ 328: (2000) 1 DMC 320

that deceased wife was meted out with ill-treatment, and offence punishable under Section 498-A of the Penal Code, 1860 was committed.[53]

3.21. ILLICIT RELATIONSHIP NOT AN OFFENCE UNDER SECTION 498-A IPC

In this case the illicit relationship appeared to be the main reason that prompted the deceased wife to commit suicide. High Court said reason cannot be a ground to convict the accused under Section 304-B of the IPC. The deceased on the apprehension of illicit relationship out of dispute committed suicide, High court held that accused could not be held guilty for an offence under Section 498-A of the IPC. Further the court observed that it is doubtful proposition to say whether mere illicit relationship simpliciter could constitute a mental cruelty within the definition of Section 498-A, the legal answer to the said hypothetical proposition is unnecessary in this case.[54]

3.22. WHEN NO EVIDENCE OF QUARREL FOUND

In this case all witnesses stated that no quarrel had taken place between appellant and his wife in their presence. High Court observed that the present case was not a case of dowry death nor the deceased having been instigated into committing suicide for her failure to satisfy the dowry

---

53. *Paparambaka Rosamma v. State of A.P.*, (1999) 7 SCC 695: 1999 SCC (Cri) 1361: 1999 SCC OnLine SC 882

54. *Vishwambar v. State of Karnataka*, 2006 SCC OnLine Kar 192: (2006) 4 Kant LJ 348: (2006) 4 AIR Kant R 306: (2006) 3 AIR Jhar R (NOC 757) 13: 2006 Cri LJ 3168: (2006) 3 KCCR (SN 177) 183

demands of the accused appellant. The prosecution utterly failed to prove its case against the accused appellant and the appellant was acquitted.[55]

3.23. BRINGING FIRST WIFE TO THE HOUSE OF SECOND WIFE

Supreme Court held that permitting the first wife to enter the house of deceased second wife with newborn child does not amounts to a cruel act as such act cannot amount to "cruelty" within the meaning of the second limb of clause (*a*) of the Explanation under Section 498-A IPC.[56]

3.24. WHEN EXTRA-MARITAL RELATIONSHIP OF HUSBAND DOES NOT AMOUNT TO CRUELTY

"Marital relationship" means the legally protected marital interest of one spouse to another which include marital obligation to another like companionship, living under the same roof, sexual relation and the exclusive enjoyment of them, to have children, their upbringing, services in the home, support, affection, love, liking and so on. Extramarital relationship as such is not defined in the Penal Code. Though, according to the prosecution in this case, it was that relationship which ultimately led to mental harassment and cruelty within the Explanation to Section 498-A and that A-1 had abetted the wife to commit suicide. Supreme Court examined whether the relationship between husband

---

55. *Mohan Singh Panwar v. State of Uttaranchal*, 2006 SCC OnLine Utt 62: 2007 Cri LJ 2069: (2007) 5 AIR Bom R (NOC 777) 291

56. *Kantilal Martaji Pandor v. State of Gujarat*, (2013) 8 SCC 781: (2013) 4 SCC (Cri) 448: 2013 SCC OnLine SC 667

of deceased and the other women amounted to mental harassment and cruelty.

Supreme Court held that the mere fact that the husband has developed some intimacy with another, during the subsistence of marriage and failed to discharge his marital obligations, as such would not amount to "cruelty", but it must be of such a nature as is likely to drive the spouse to commit suicide to fall within the Explanation to Section 498-A IPC. Harassment, of course, need not be in the form of physical assault and even mental harassment also would come within the purview of Section 498-A IPC. Mental cruelty, of course, varies from person to person, depending upon the intensity and the degree of endurance, some may meet with courage and some others suffer in silence, to some it may be unbearable and a weak person may think of ending one's life. Supreme Court, found that the alleged extramarital relationship was not of such a nature as to drive the wife to commit suicide or that accused husband had ever intended or acted in such a manner which under normal circumstances, would drive the wife to commit suicide.[57]

In another case, there was some evidence about the illicit relationship and even if the same is proven, supreme court was of the considered opinion that cruelty, as envisaged under the first limb of Section 498-A IPC would not get attracted. It would be difficult to hold that the mental cruelty was of such a degree that it would drive the wife to commit suicide. Mere extra-marital relationship, even if proved, would be illegal and immoral, as has been

---

57. *Pinakin Mahipatray Rawal v. State of Gujarat,* (2013) 10 SCC 48: (2013) 4 SCC (Civ) 616: (2013) 3 SCC (Cri) 801: 2013 SCC OnLine SC 814

said in *Pinakin Mahipatray Rawal* [*Pinakin Mahipatray Rawal v. State of Gujarat*, (2013) 10 SCC 48: (2013) 4 SCC (Civ) 616: (2013) 3 SCC (Cri) 801], but it would take a different character if the prosecution brings some evidence on record to show that the accused had conducted in such a manner to drive the wife to commit suicide. In the instant case, the accused may have been involved in an illicit relationship with Appellant 4, but in the absence of some other acceptable evidence on record that can establish such high degree of mental cruelty, the Explanation to Section 498-A IPC which includes cruelty to drive a woman to commit suicide, would not be attracted.[58]

3.25. WHEN THE COMPLAINT BY SECOND WIFE NOT MAINTAINABLE

If a person enters into a second marriage without legally dissolving the first, the second marriage is considered void under Hindu law. This principle has been upheld by the constitutional courts also. Section 498A addresses the menace of cruelty by a husband or his relatives. The term "husband" implies a legally valid marriage. In cases where the marriage is void, the applicability of Section 498A becomes doubtful. If a woman conceals her existing marriage and contracts a second marriage with another person then the complaint under section 498 A IPC agaisnt the second husband will not be maintainable. The term "husband" in Section 498A IPC could include a person who enters into a marital relationship with a woman, so when the marraige itself is void 498 A IPC will be inapplicable.

---

58. *Ghusabhai Raisangbhai Chorasiya v. State of Gujarat*, (2015) 11 SCC 753: (2015) 4 SCC (Cri) 545: 2015 SCC OnLine SC 137

Section 498A IPC applies to "husband or relative of husband of a woman subjecting her to cruelty." The term "husband" here refers to a legally wedded husband.

Since the second wife (married during the subsitence of first marriage) does not have the status of a legally wedded wife, she **cannot be considered the "wife"** for the purpose of Section 498A IPC.

Complaint under section Section 498-A IPC is not maintainable against husband if the case is filed by his second wife when the marriage with first wife still subsist.[59]

---

59. Akhilesh Keshari and 3 ors vs. State of U.P and Anr, APPLICATION U/S 482 No. - 38288 of 2023, Neutral Citation No. - 2024:AHC:54046

CHAPTER 4

ALLEGATION OF UN-NATURAL SEX BY WIFE UNDER SECTION 377 IPC

4.1 INTRODUCTION

The Section 377 IPC is a colonial-era law that criminalizes "carnal intercourse against the order of nature" between two or more individuals. The punishment includes imprisonment for life or up to 10 years, along with a fine.

The Delhi High Court in Naz Foundation case[60] declared that Section 377 IPC, insofar it criminalises consensual sexual acts of adults in private, is violative of Articles 21, 14 and 15 of the Constitution. Therefore Section 377 was partially struck down, but the decision was later challenged.

Subsequently Supreme Court held that law could only be changed by Parliament and not by courts and overruled the decision in Naz Foundation (supra).

Thereafter again the matter invited the attention of the Supreme Court of India and in the matter of Navtej Singh Johar v. Union of India, A five-judge Constitution Bench unanimously struck down Section 377 IPC insofar as it criminalized consensual same-sex relations and therefore the decision in the matter of Naz Foundation (supra) was affirmed. The judgment did not decriminalize non-

---

60. Naz Foundation vs. Government of NCT of Delhi, **2009 SCC OnLine Del 1762: (2009) 111 DRJ 1 (DB): (2009) 160 DLT 277 (DB): (2010) 2 AIR Kant R (NOC 149) 60: 2010 Cri LJ 94: (2009) 2 MWN (Cri) 336: (2009) 3 CCR 1**

consensual acts, bestiality, or sexual offenses involving minors, which remained punishable under the law.

4.2 UNDERSTANDING UN-NATURAL SEX

Section 377 IPC state as under:

Unnatural offences.—Whoever voluntarily has carnal intercourse against the order of nature with any man, woman or animal, shall be punished with [2][imprisonment for life], or with imprisonment of either description for a term which may extend to ten years, and shall also be liable to fine.

Explanation.—Penetration is sufficient to constitute the carnal intercourse necessary to the offence described in this section.]

It is to be noted that under section 377 IPC a carnal intercourse against the order of nature is punishable. Therefore it becomes important to understand as to what is the order of nature. Order of nature here means using the bodily organ for the purpose God/nature has created it.

4.3 UN-NATURAL SEX BETWEEN HUSBAND AND WIFE IS NOT AN OFFENCE.

The question, whether offence under Sections 376 and 377 of the IPC is attracted looking to the facts and circumstances of the case when the accused and the victim were the husband and wife ?, arose before the High Court of Chattisgarh in Gorakhnth Sharma's case.[61]

---

61. Gorakhnth Sharma vs. State of Chattisgarh, CRA No. 891 of 2019, 2025 LiveLaw (Chh) 16

The Chattisgarh high court observed that the From perusal of Section 375, 376 and 377 IPC it is quite vivid that in view of amended definition of Section 375 IPC, offence under Section 377 IPC between husband and wife has no place and, as such rape cannot be made out. It is pertinent to mention here that in the amendment in Section 375 IPC in the year 2013, Exception- 2 has been provided which speaks that sexual intercourse or sexual acts by a man with his own wife is not a rape and therefore if any unnatural sex as defined under section 377 is committed by the husband with his wife, then it can also not be treated to be an offence. It is quite vivid that Section 377 i.e. unnatural sex is not well equipped and offender is not defined therein but body parts are well defined, which are also included in Section 375 i.e. carnal intercourse against the order of nature. while considering the constitutionality of Section 377 IPC criminalizes 'carnal intercourse against the order of nature' which among other things has been interpreted to include oral and anal sex. Obviously, Section 377 of IPC is not well equipped as unnatural offence has also not been defined anywhere. The five- judge Bench of the Hon'ble Supreme Court in Navtej Singh Johar while testing the constitutionality of said provision has held that some parts of Section 377 are unconstitutional and finally held that if unnatural offence is done with consent then offence of Section 377 IPC is not made out.[62]

The court further observed in this case[63] that considering the said legal position and in the light of

---

62. Gorakhnth Sharma vs. State of Chattisgarh, CRA No. 891 of 2019, 2025 LiveLaw (Chh) 16

63. Gorakhnth Sharma vs. State of Chattisgarh, CRA No. 891 of 2019, 2025 LiveLaw (Chh) 16

amended definition of Section 375 and the relationship for which exception provided for not taking consent i.e. between husband & wife and not making offence of Section 376, it is quite vivid that the definition of rape as provided under Section 375 includes penetration of penis in the parts of the body i.e. vagina, urethra or anus of a woman for which consent is not required then unnatural sex cannot be made as unnatural offence between husband and wife, as such apparently, there is repugnancy in these two situations in the light of definition of Section 375 and unnatural offence of Section 377. It is also well settled principle of law that if the provisions of latter enactment are so inconsistent or repugnant to the provisions of an earlier one then the two cannot stand together and earlier is abrogated by the latter. Thus, it is quite clear that at the same time, as per the definition of Section 375 of IPC, the offender is classified as a 'man'. Here in the present case, the appellant is a 'husband' and victim is a 'woman' and here she is a 'wife' and parts of the body which are used for carnal intercourse are also common, therefore, the offence between husband and wife cannot be made out under Section 375 IPC as per the repeal made by way of amendment and in view of repugnancy between both the sections. It is quite vivid that when everything is repealed under Section 375 of IPC then how offence under Section 377 of IPC would be attracted if it is committed between husband and wife. The Hon'ble Supreme Court in the case of **Navtej Singh Johar and others vs. Union of India through Secretary, Ministry of law and justice 2018(10) SCC 1** has considered the provisions of Section 375, 376 and 377 and held as under:

"268.11. A cursory reading of both Section 375 and 377 IPC reveals that although the former section gives due recognition to the absence of "wilful and informed consent" for an act to be termed as rape, per contra, Section 377 does not contain any such qualification embodying in itself the absence of "wilful and informed consent" to criminalise carnal intercourse which consequently results in criminalising even voluntary carnal intercourse between homosexuals, heterosexuals, bisexuals and transgenders. Section 375 IPC, after the coming into force of the Criminal Law (Amendment) Act, 2013 has not used the words "subject to any other provision of the IPC". This indicates that Section 375 IPC is not subject to Section 377 IPC. 268.12. The expression "against the order of nature" has neither been defined in Section 377 IPC nor in any other provision of the IPC. The connotation given to the expression by various judicial pronouncements includes all sexual acts which are not intended for the purpose of procreation. Therefore, if coitus is not performed for procreation only, it does not per se make it "against the order of nature."

Thus, it is quite vivid, that if the age of wife is not below age of 15 years then any sexual intercourse or sexual act by the husband with her wife cannot be termed as rape under the circumstances, as such absence of consent of wife for unnatural act loses its importance, therefore, this Court is of the considered opinion that the offence under Section 376 and 377 of the IPC against the appellant is not made out.[64]

---

64. Gorakhnth Sharma vs. State of Chattisgarh, CRA No. 891 of 2019, 2025 LiveLaw (Chh) 16